Trey Cox & Alan Dabdoub

In-House Counsel's Compass

Navigating Privilege, Immunity, and Risk in Texas and Beyond

First published by Cox Advocacy Publishing 2026

First edition

Table of Contents

Introduction

"An ounce of prevention is worth a pound of cure." – *Benjamin Franklin*

The role of the general counsel has never been more complex, consequential, or perilous. Once viewed primarily as mere middlemen, today's in-house lawyers must be strategic partners, risk managers, and defenders of corporate integrity—all while navigating an increasingly hostile litigation and regulatory landscape.

Nowhere are the stakes higher than in the doctrines that protect candid advice and legal strategy—privilege and work product—in the immunity that shields the lawyer who gives that advice, and in the personal exposure that increasingly shadows the role. These protections are the lifejackets of effective legal practice: they enable candid communication, preserve strategic preparation, and shield lawyers from personal liability. Yet they are also fragile, inconsistently applied across jurisdictions, and easily lost through inadvertence or missteps.

This book is a practical guide for Texas general counsel—and the litigation attorneys advising them—on how to protect privilege, preserve work product, run internal investigations and data breach responses without forfeiting either, govern the records that artificial intelligence now creates, minimize personal liability, and navigate immunity doctrines in Texas and beyond. It is not a theoretical treatise. It is a field guide, informed by experience and built to equip lawyers with practical strategies for high-stakes disputes.

The chapters move in four arcs. The first establishes the two doctrines on which everything else depends: the attorney-client privilege, the bedrock of candid communication and the protection most easily lost, and the work-product doctrine, the shield for a lawyer's preparation, strategy, and intellectual capital.

The second arc carries those doctrines into the three settings where modern companies most often lose them: the internal investigation, where privilege is won or forfeited early; the data breach, where the forensic report is at once the most useful document and the most contested; and the use of artificial intelligence, where prompts and outputs are quietly becoming records the other side will demand.

The third arc turns to the lawyer's own position—the growing risk that in-house counsel become defendants and witnesses, and the attorney immunity that, in Texas, offers broad but bounded protection against claims by non-clients.

The fourth arc addresses the cross-border reality, in which a company operating across state and national lines must reconcile inconsistent privilege and immunity regimes and assume the strictest standard will govern.

Together, these chapters provide a practical guide for navigating the terrain of modern in-house litigation practice.

Chapter 1

The Core of Attorney-Client Privilege in Texas

"Trust is built in drops and lost in buckets." – Kevin Plank, founder of Under Armour

Attorney-client privilege is the bedrock of corporate legal counsel. It lets business leaders consult their lawyers candidly, confident that the disclosure will not later be used as evidence against them. For the Texas general counsel, understanding the privilege's scope, its limits, and the ways it fails is not optional—it is survival. This chapter is a practice-oriented map of the privilege under Texas Rule of Evidence 503, with particular attention to the dual-role environment that defines in-house practice and produces most of its privilege risk.

The Law

Texas Rule of Evidence 503 codifies the attorney-client privilege. It protects confidential communications made to facilitate the rendition of professional legal services between a client and the client's lawyer or their representatives. The rule reads simply; its application is anything but. Courts look past the label on a document to its substance—the role the lawyer was playing, the purpose of the communication, and who else was in the room. *See Univ. of Tex. Sys. v. Franklin Ctr. for Gov't & Pub. Integrity*, 675 S.W.3d 273, 281–87 (Tex. 2023).

Three principles govern, and each is a place the privilege can fail.

First, the privilege protects communications, not facts. A client cannot shield a fact from discovery by reciting it to a lawyer; the underlying fact remains discoverable even when the communication conveying it does not. An executive who tells the general counsel what happened has not made the event itself privileged—only the communication.

Second, the privilege attaches only when the lawyer is acting as a lawyer. A communication seeking or rendering legal advice is protected; one seeking or giving business advice is not. When a single communication does both—the daily reality for in-house counsel—Texas asks whether obtaining or providing legal advice was a significant purpose of the communication, not merely an incidental one. *See Franklin Ctr.*, 675 S.W.3d at 281–87. That test is forgiving in theory and unforgiving in practice, because the party claiming privilege must show, from the record, that legal advice was a genuine purpose and not a label applied after the fact.

Third, the privilege requires confidentiality, and confidentiality is lost by disclosure. A communication shared beyond the circle of those who need it to obtain or deliver the legal advice—an outside consultant, an auditor, a public-relations firm—ordinarily forfeits the protection, unless that third party was retained by counsel to assist in the legal advice and the arrangement is documented. The chapter on internal investigations takes up that consultant problem in detail.

Who is "the client" inside a corporation? The Supreme Court answered in *Upjohn Co. v. United States*, rejecting the narrow "control group" test—which had confined the privilege to communications with senior management—in favor of a broader subject-matter standard. 449 U.S. 383, 393 (1981). Texas follows the modern approach. *See In re Monsanto Co.*, 998 S.W.2d 917, 922 (Tex. App.—Waco 1999, orig. proceeding). Under it, the privilege reaches communications with employees at any level when they act at the direction of corporate superiors, communicate about matters within the scope of their duties, and do so to secure legal advice for the company. That breadth matters most in investigations, where the people who hold the facts are rarely the people in the C-suite. It is not universal, however: some states still apply the control-group test, so a company litigating across state lines cannot assume the broad Texas-federal rule will travel, as the cross-border chapter explains.

The rule also defines who, within the company, can speak for it. A "representative of the client" under Rule 503(a) includes not only those authorized to obtain or act on legal advice for the corporation but also any employee who makes or receives a confidential communication while acting within the scope of employment. *See* Tex. R. Evid. 503(a)(2). That definition is what makes the subject-matter test workable in practice: the line employee interviewed by counsel speaks as a representative of the client, so the communication is the company's to protect or to waive.

Finally, the privilege has limits written into the rule itself. Rule 503(d) lists exceptions, and the most dangerous to a corporation is the crime-fraud exception: no privilege exists for a communication made to enable or aid anyone to commit or plan what the client knew or reasonably should have known was a crime or fraud. *See* Tex. R. Evid. 503(d)(1). The line is principled but easy to cross in practice. Advice about whether contemplated conduct is lawful is privileged; a communication that enlists the lawyer in furthering the misconduct is not. A general counsel who understands the difference protects the privilege; one who blurs it can forfeit it precisely when the company needs it most.

How Companies Lose

The most common privilege dispute facing a general counsel is not whether a document exists. It is whether the lawyer was acting as a lawyer when it was created.

Consider the ordinary exchange. A CEO emails the general counsel: "What do you think of raising prices ten percent in Q3?" Counsel replies: "If we raise prices, we risk antitrust scrutiny given our market share; from a legal perspective, we should document a legitimate business justification." The second clause is legal advice and is privileged. The first—an opinion about pricing—is business advice and is not. When the two intertwine in a single email, opposing counsel will argue that the communication's purpose was business strategy and the legal gloss incidental. The company's ability to defend the privilege turns on whether the record shows legal advice was a significant purpose. Write the email so that it does.

From that root grow the three ways companies lose the privilege they assumed they had.

The first is disclosure to a third party. When confidential communications travel outside the attorney-client relationship—looping in a consultant, forwarding to an auditor, copying a public-relations adviser—the privilege ordinarily evaporates. Picture a general counsel who shares a candid memorandum assessing the company's legal exposure with its outside auditor to support a financial-statement position. The instinct is reasonable; the consequence is that the memo, now disclosed to a third party, may be discoverable in the litigation that follows, exposing counsel's own risk assessment to the adversary. Unless the third party was retained through counsel to assist in delivering legal advice, and the file documents it, the inclusion is a waiver.

The second is offensive use. A company waives the privilege when it puts its own legal advice at issue, most often by asserting an advice-of-counsel defense. The Texas Supreme Court framed the doctrine in *Republic Insurance Co. v. Davis*: a litigant may not use the privilege as both a sword and a shield, wielding favorable privileged material to gain advantage while withholding the rest. 856 S.W.2d 158, 163 (Tex. 1993). The waiver is not surgical. Once the subject is opened, it opens for the entire subject matter, and the adversary gains discovery into every related communication. Asserting advice of counsel is an all-in wager—make it deliberately, not reflexively.

The third is inadvertence. In large productions, privileged documents slip through. Texas Rule of Civil Procedure 193.3(d) provides a "snap-back": a party may claw back inadvertently produced privileged material if it asserts the privilege promptly after discovering the disclosure. "Promptly" means days, not weeks. A general counsel without a rapid-response protocol to catch, assert, and recover an inadvertent production is one careless vendor away from an avoidable waiver.

The cost is concrete. Picture a whistleblower suit alleging fraud. In discovery, the court rules that a chain of emails between the general counsel and the CFO is not privileged because it blended legal and business advice. The emails become trial exhibits and are read to the jury. The defense narrative buckles, and the general counsel's credibility goes with it. This is not a far-fetched scenario; courts have grown skeptical of overbroad privilege claims, and adversaries press the point hard. *See Attorney General v. Facebook, Inc.*, 164 N.E.3d 873, 886 (Mass. 2021).

Strategic Guidance

Privilege is preserved by discipline applied before any dispute, not by argument after one begins.

Write for the record. Mark genuinely legal communications "PRIVILEGED AND CONFIDENTIAL: ATTORNEY-CLIENT COMMUNICATION"—not reflexively on everything, which dilutes the designation, but on communications that actually seek or deliver legal advice. Labels are not dispositive, but consistent, honest labeling helps a court find the communication's purpose.

Segregate legal from business advice. Where you can, deliver legal risk assessments in a channel distinct from business commentary, so that a single document does not force a court to untangle the two. When they must coexist, make the legal purpose explicit in the text rather than leaving it to inference.

Manage the third-party perimeter. Bring consultants, auditors, and other outside advisers inside the privilege only when they are retained through counsel to assist the legal advice, and paper the arrangement at the outset rather than reconstructing it under subpoena.

Assert the privilege precisely. When privileged material is withheld in discovery, Texas requires a withholding statement and, on request, a log describing what is withheld and the basis for the claim. *See* Tex. R. Civ. P. 193.3(a)–(b). Two failures recur: a boilerplate log that describes nothing, which invites a motion to compel, and over-designation—marking everything privileged—which teaches the court to distrust the entire log. A precise, honest log is not a clerical chore; it is often the difference between a privilege claim a court will sustain and one it will pierce.

Embed the discipline in the organization. The legal department cannot hold the line alone. The most effective general counsel install written privilege policies—when to involve legal, how to label, when to pick up the phone instead of sending an email—train senior leaders on the legal-versus-business distinction, and designate a privilege liaison in each business unit. And they keep a rapid-response protocol ready for the inadvertent production, because the snap-back rule rewards speed.

Key Takeaways

The privilege protects communications, not facts, and only when the lawyer is acting as a lawyer; in the dual-role world of in-house practice, the controlling question is whether legal advice was a significant purpose of the communication—and the record must show it. *See Franklin Ctr.*, 675 S.W.3d at 281–87.

Inside a corporation, the privilege reaches employees at any level under the subject-matter test, *Upjohn*, 449 U.S. at 393, but that breadth may not survive in states that still apply the control-group test, so cross-border matters demand caution.

The privilege is not absolute: the crime-fraud exception withdraws it from communications made to further what the client knew or should have known was a crime or fraud. *See* Tex. R. Evid. 503(d)(1).

Disclosure to a third party outside the legal-advice circle ordinarily waives the privilege, and offensive use waives it across the entire subject matter; bring consultants inside only through counsel, and assert advice of counsel only as a deliberate, all-in choice. *See Republic Ins. Co. v. Davis*, 856 S.W.2d at 163.

Inadvertent production is the most common waiver and the most preventable; Rule 193.3(d) rewards a fast claw-back, so keep a rapid-response protocol in place—and treat the privilege as a strategic asset guarded by routine discipline, because it is tested not in the abstract but word by word in discovery.

Chapter 2
The Work-Product Doctrine in Texas

"An attorney's thoughts, heretofore inviolate, would not be his own." – Hickman v. Taylor, 329 U.S. 495 (1947)

If the attorney-client privilege protects confidential communications, the work-product doctrine protects the lawyer's preparation. Privilege guards what the client and lawyer say to each other; work product guards the lawyer's notes, theories, and strategy from being handed to the opposition. For a general counsel, the doctrine is not an academic refinement. It is what keeps an internal investigation, a litigation risk assessment, and a trial plan out of the adversary's hands—when it is invoked correctly, and only then.

The Law

The doctrine traces to *Hickman v. Taylor*, where the Supreme Court recognized that a lawyer's mental processes must remain private for the adversarial system to function; without that protection, lawyers would stop committing their analysis to paper, and advocacy would suffer. 329 U.S. 495, 510–11 (1947). Texas codifies the principle in Rule of Civil Procedure 192.5, which protects material prepared in anticipation of litigation and sorts it into two tiers.

Core work product—an attorney's mental impressions, opinions, conclusions, and legal theories—is absolutely protected. No showing of need, however strong, compels its disclosure; one lawyer's analysis does not become the other side's evidence. *See In re Nat'l Lloyds Ins. Co.*, 532 S.W.3d 794, 804 (Tex. 2017). Non-core, or factual, work product—witness-interview summaries, event chronologies, documents assembled for the case—occupies a weaker position. An opponent can reach it by showing both a substantial need for the material and an undue hardship in obtaining the substantial equivalent elsewhere. *Id.* A company that interviews witnesses right after a catastrophe holds non-core work product; if those witnesses later vanish or refuse to cooperate, a court may order the summaries produced.

Everything turns on the phrase "in anticipation of litigation," and Texas defines it precisely. Under *National Tank Co. v. Brotherton*, a document is prepared in anticipation of litigation when two conditions are met: objectively, a reasonable person in the party's position would have concluded, from the totality of the circumstances, that there was a substantial chance litigation would ensue; and subjectively, the party resisting discovery believed in good faith that litigation would result and created the document for that purpose. 851 S.W.2d 193, 204 (Tex. 1993). "Substantial chance" does not mean a lawsuit was certain or even imminent—but it means more than the abstract possibility that hangs over every business.

That subjective prong is where dual-purpose documents come apart. Much of what a company creates serves a business need that would exist whether or not litigation loomed—a safety review, an incident report, a compliance file. A document like that does not become work product merely because litigation was also on the horizon; the question is whether it was prepared because of the prospect of litigation, in a form it would not otherwise have taken. The adversary's first move is always the same: argue the document was generated in the ordinary course of business, where no protection attaches. The party claiming work product must be able to answer that the litigation purpose is what brought the document into being.

One last point of orientation: work product and the attorney-client privilege overlap but are not the same, and the difference is useful. Privilege protects a confidential lawyer-client communication whether or not litigation is in view; work product protects material prepared because litigation is anticipated, including things that are not communications at all—a lawyer's notes, a chronology, an interview summary, a consultant's analysis. A single document may carry both protections, one, or neither. The lesson is to claim each where it fits, because they fail differently: disclosing a document to an aligned party may forfeit the privilege while leaving the work-product protection intact, and a document that is not a privileged communication may still be shielded as work product. Assert both, and the court has two independent grounds to deny discovery.

How Companies Lose

The doctrine fails most often not through a dramatic waiver but through a document that never qualified for protection in the first place.

Compare two investigations. A trucking company's general counsel, hours after a fatal crash, directs outside experts to interview witnesses, photograph the scene, and prepare a report; the file documents that litigation was anticipated and counsel ran the work. That report is work product. Now take a chemical company's annual safety audit, performed on a routine schedule long before any incident. After an explosion, the company recasts the latest audit as litigation preparation and claims protection. A court will see through it: the audit was an ordinary-course business record made before litigation was anticipated, and no after-the-fact label converts it into work product. The line between the two is thin, and it is drawn by purpose and timing, not by the stamp on the cover page.

The same trap recurs across the enterprise. A workplace investigation that human resources runs as routine compliance produces discoverable business records; the identical investigation, directed by counsel because litigation is anticipated, produces work product. An outside engineer retained by the operations team to evaluate a product generates a discoverable report; the same engineer retained through counsel to assist the litigation defense may not. Even the first-party insurer's claim file turns on this distinction—whether the investigation was the ordinary business of adjusting a claim or was conducted because litigation had become substantially likely. *See In re Nat'l Lloyds Ins. Co.*, 532 S.W.3d at 804–06.

Then there is waiver of work product that did qualify. The most common form is selective disclosure—handing a regulator or adversary the favorable portions while withholding the rest. Courts reject the sword-and-shield maneuver. *See Republic Ins. Co. v. Davis*, 856 S.W.2d 158, 163 (Tex. 1993); *In re Kubosh Bail Bonding*, 522 S.W.3d 75, 89 (Tex. App.—Houston [1st Dist.] 2017, orig. proceeding). A subtler waiver runs through expert witnesses: Texas treats a testifying expert's file as broadly discoverable, so work product shared with a testifying expert in connection with the opinions generally loses its protection. *See* Tex. R. Civ. P. 192.3(e). Disclosure to a third party not aligned in the litigation, and production without a claw-back protocol, will likewise forfeit the doctrine.

Consider how a single early decision compounds. A manufacturer learns of a possible defect and, sensing trouble, has its quality team prepare a detailed root-cause analysis—no lawyer involved, no anticipation of litigation documented. Months later the suits arrive. The analysis, created in the ordinary course, is not work product; it is produced, and it becomes the centerpiece of the plaintiffs' case, quoted in every brief and waved before the jury as the company's own admission. Had counsel been brought in at the first sign of trouble, directed the analysis as part of assessing legal exposure, and documented the anticipation of litigation, the same investigation might have stayed protected. The distance between catastrophe and protection was a choice made in the first week.

The stakes explain the discipline. Work product is where a company's candor lives—the unvarnished assessment of what went wrong, what it might cost, and how exposed the company truly is. When that material is produced, it does not merely add documents to a pile; it hands the adversary a roadmap drawn by the company's own lawyers. The post-incident report becomes the plaintiff's liability theory. The early risk memo becomes the damages demand. And the lawyer who wrote candidly, expecting protection, becomes the witness asked to read it aloud. That is why the doctrine repays the procedural care it demands.

Strategic Guidance

Work product is earned by the way the work is set up, not by the label added later.

Establish and document the anticipation trigger. The single most valuable habit is a short, contemporaneous record—dated when litigation first became substantially likely—stating that the ensuing investigation is being conducted at counsel's direction because litigation is anticipated. That record is what satisfies *National Tank*'s two prongs months later, when memory has faded and the adversary insists the work was routine.

Run sensitive investigations through counsel. Where protection matters, counsel should direct the investigation in fact, not merely receive its output. Engagement letters with consultants and experts should state that they are retained to assist counsel in rendering legal advice and preparing for litigation, and the engagement should run through the legal department. Keep a clear wall between a consultant retained to help defend litigation and an expert later designated to testify, because crossing that line can convert protected analysis into discoverable material.

Label, but do not rely on labels. Mark genuine work product "Attorney Work Product—Prepared in Anticipation of Litigation." Consistent labeling is persuasive evidence of intent, but it is not dispositive; a label on an ordinary-course document will not save it, and its absence will not doom a document that was truly prepared for litigation.

Use common-interest agreements with care. Texas recognizes a common-interest or allied-litigant doctrine that can let aligned parties share protected materials without waiver, but the Texas Supreme Court has construed it narrowly. *See In re XL Specialty Ins. Co.*, 373 S.W.3d 46 (Tex. 2012). Paper the arrangement, define the shared legal interest precisely, and do not assume the doctrine reaches further than it does.

Bring the litigation hold inside the doctrine and embed the habit in the organization. State that the hold is issued under legal direction and in anticipation of litigation, so that preservation memos and custodian instructions travel under work-product protection. Train managers that the instinct after any serious incident is to call legal before generating reports, standardize investigation templates with proper headers, and keep a legal-led rapid-response team so that the earliest and most sensitive documents are created inside the doctrine rather than outside it.

Key Takeaways

Work product divides into core material—mental impressions and legal theories, absolutely protected—and non-core factual material, which an opponent can reach on a showing of substantial need and undue hardship. *See In re Nat'l Lloyds Ins. Co.*, 532 S.W.3d at 804.

Protection exists only for material prepared in anticipation of litigation, which in Texas requires both an objective substantial chance of litigation and a subjective, good-faith purpose of preparing for it; a dual-purpose document is protected only if the litigation purpose is what brought it into being. *See National Tank Co. v. Brotherton*, 851 S.W.2d at 204.

The most common failure is not waiver but a document that never qualified—a routine audit or ordinary-course report dressed up as litigation preparation after the fact.

Selective disclosure forfeits the protection, and so does sharing work product with a testifying expert; courts will not let a party use favorable work product as a sword while shielding the rest. *See Republic Ins. Co. v. Davis*, 856 S.W.2d at 163; Tex. R. Civ. P. 192.3(e).

Earn the protection up front: document the moment litigation becomes substantially likely, route the investigation through counsel, retain consultants to assist counsel, and treat labels as helpful evidence of intent rather than a substitute for it.

Chapter 3

Privilege During Internal Investigations, Crises, and Government Investigations

"Sunlight is said to be the best of disinfectants; electric light the most efficient policeman." — Louis D. Brandeis, Other People's Money and How the Bankers Use It (1914)

Brandeis was right about sunlight, and the plaintiffs' bar and the government agree with him. Regulators, whistleblowers, and opposing counsel all believe the company's internal findings belong in the open. The general counsel's job, when an investigation begins, is to decide—deliberately, and before it is too late—what belongs in the light and what stays protected.

No moment tests privilege harder than the internal investigation. This is when the company gathers its worst facts, often fast, often while regulators and plaintiffs are already circling. The work is valuable precisely because it is candid, and candor is exactly what an adversary wants to read. Whether the investigation file stays protected almost never turns on the word "Privileged" stamped at the top. It turns on three things: the purpose for which the work was done, the structure through which it was done, and the discipline with which it was handled.

The stakes have risen. Companies now run more investigations than ever—harassment and retaliation complaints, whistleblower reports, regulatory inquiries, ESG and accounting questions, data incidents. More of these unfold alongside parallel litigation or enforcement, which means the investigation file is no longer an internal document; it is a discovery target from the day it is created. A general counsel who treats an investigation casually hands the other side a roadmap. A general counsel who treats it as a privileged legal undertaking, from the first hour, keeps control.

The Law

The threshold question is purpose. Did the company conduct the investigation to obtain or provide legal advice, or to satisfy a business or compliance function it would have performed regardless? Privilege protects the former. It does not reach the latter merely because a lawyer was in the room.

Texas Rule of Evidence 503 supplies the framework. It protects confidential communications made to facilitate the rendition of legal services, and—critically for investigations—it reaches communications among the lawyer's representatives, not just the lawyer and the client. *See* Tex. R. Evid. 503(a)(2), (b). That matters because modern investigations are rarely conducted by a single lawyer asking questions. They are conducted by teams: in-house counsel, outside counsel, and the non-lawyer consultants those lawyers engage to help.

The Texas Supreme Court confirmed how far that protection extends in *Univ. of Tex. Sys. v. Franklin Ctr. for Gov't & Pub. Integrity*, 675 S.W.3d 273 (Tex. 2023). The University retained Kroll, a non-lawyer investigative firm, to examine its admissions practices, and the question was whether the privilege covered Kroll's work. The Court held that it did. Privilege shields communications with an independent third party retained for the significant purpose of assisting counsel in rendering legal services. *Id.* at 281–87. The protection does not depend on a formal employment relationship, and it does not hinge on whether the engagement letter recited the magic words "privileged" or "legal advice." The analysis focuses on the purpose and confidentiality of the communications, not on contractual formalities. For a general counsel deciding how to staff an investigation, *Franklin Center* is the most important Texas privilege decision in a generation.

The corporate-client framework comes from the United States Supreme Court's decision in *Upjohn Co. v. United States*, 449 U.S. 383 (1981). *Upjohn* rejected the cramped "control group" rule and held that the privilege protects communications between counsel and employees throughout the organization when those communications are made to help the company obtain legal advice. *Id.* at 389–97. *Upjohn* is also the source of the warning that bears its name—the explanation a company lawyer gives an employee that the lawyer represents the company, not the employee personally. The case did not mandate any particular script, but the practice it inspired is now the dividing line between a clean investigation and a messy one.

Federal law has converged on a sensible test for the dual-purpose investigation. In *In re Kellogg Brown & Root, Inc.*, 756 F.3d 754 (D.C. Cir. 2014), then-Judge Kavanaugh held that an internal investigation does not lose privilege simply because the company also had business or regulatory reasons to conduct it. "So long as obtaining or providing legal advice was one of the significant purposes of the internal investigation, the attorney-client privilege applies"—even if there were other purposes, and even if the investigation was required by corporate policy or regulation. *Id.* at 758–60, *cert. denied*, 136 S. Ct. 823 (2016). The court added what *Franklin Center* would later echo: nothing requires a company to use magic words to secure the privilege. The convergence is useful. Texas focuses on whether assisting counsel was a "significant purpose"; the leading federal authority asks whether legal advice was "one of the significant purposes." A general counsel who can answer yes, and prove it, is on solid ground in either forum.

The hard case is the genuinely dual-purpose investigation—the inquiry the company would have run anyway for compliance or operational reasons, now also routed through counsel. The more an investigation looks like routine business the company performs in the ordinary course, the more exposed the privilege claim. This is not a reason to avoid investigating. It is a reason to establish the legal purpose at the outset and to document it.

One doctrine rarely travels alone. Investigation materials prepared in anticipation of litigation may also be protected work product, independent of the privilege. The two doctrines overlap but are not identical, and the work-product analysis turns on the anticipation-of-litigation standard discussed in the preceding chapter—whether a reasonable person would have anticipated litigation when the document was created. *See National Tank Co. v. Brotherton*, 851 S.W.2d 193, 204 (Tex. 1993). Treat privilege and work product as belt and suspenders. Claim both where both apply.

How Companies Lose

Privilege is lost in predictable ways. Each of them is avoidable.

No warning. A company lawyer interviews an employee, the employee assumes the lawyer is looking out for him, and later—when interests diverge—he claims a personal privilege over the conversation or accuses the company of misleading him. Without a documented Upjohn warning, the company is left arguing about what was said in a room with no record. The warning is cheap. Its absence is expensive.

The wrong frame. A complaint comes in, and the company opens a routine fact-finding through human resources or compliance. Lawyers are brought in only after the file is half-built. By then the early interviews, notes, and summaries were created for an ordinary business purpose, and no later relabeling makes them privileged. The frame is set at the beginning, not at the moment litigation arrives.

The report that travels. Counsel produces a careful written report and the company, proud of it, circulates it to the board, the business units that need to fix the problem, and the outside auditors who ask for it. Each new recipient erodes the confidentiality the privilege requires and, worse, hands a future plaintiff a single document that organizes the company's worst facts. A report can be the right tool. An over-distributed report is a liability.

The cooperation trap. The company decides to cooperate with a regulator and produces privileged investigation materials, often believing a confidentiality agreement with the agency will keep the materials away from private plaintiffs. It generally will not. Most federal circuits reject "selective waiver": disclosure of privileged material to the government waives the privilege as to everyone, including the civil litigants who follow. *See In re Columbia/HCA Healthcare Corp. Billing Practices Litig.*, 293 F.3d 289, 302 (6th Cir. 2002); *Westinghouse Elec. Corp. v. Republic of the Philippines*, 951 F.2d 1414, 1425 (3d Cir. 1991). A promise of confidentiality from the agency usually does not save it either. *See In re Pacific Pictures Corp.*, 679 F.3d 1121 (9th Cir. 2012). Disclosure to the government is, in most courts, disclosure to the world.

The unstructured crisis vendor. In a crisis, the company hires a public-relations or crisis-communications firm and folds it into legal strategy without any structure. Unlike the consultant in *Franklin Center*, this vendor was not retained for the significant purpose of assisting counsel, and looping it into privileged discussions can waive the privilege rather than extend it.

Consider how these failures compound. A manager forwards a harassment complaint to HR, which interviews witnesses and writes a summary. A week later the complainant lawyers up. Now the interview notes were created for a business purpose, no one gave an Upjohn warning, and the well-meaning summary email to the CEO—"here's what we found"—becomes the plaintiff's first exhibit. Nothing about that sequence was malicious. All of it was preventable.

Strategic Guidance

Winning the privilege fight is mostly a matter of doing a few things deliberately, and early.

Establish purpose in writing on day one. Open every significant investigation with a short scope memorandum from counsel stating that the company is conducting the inquiry to obtain legal advice. This is not boilerplate; it is the document that anchors the privilege claim months later. Where outside counsel or a consultant is engaged, the engagement should say the same thing—not as magic words, which the law does not require, but as honest evidence of a purpose that is in fact legal.

Let counsel direct the work in fact. Privilege follows substance, not titles. Counsel should set the investigation's scope, choose its witnesses, and direct any consultants. If a non-lawyer is running the investigation and a lawyer is merely cc'd, the privilege claim is thin no matter what the engagement letter says.

Warn every witness, and document it. Deliver an Upjohn warning at the start of each interview and note that you gave it. A workable script:

- I am a lawyer for [the Company]. I represent the Company, not you personally.

- This conversation is privileged, but the privilege belongs to the Company, not to you. The Company alone decides whether to waive it.

- Keep this conversation confidential.

- Do you understand, and are you willing to proceed?

Control the writing. Decide, before the work is done, what will be written and who will see it. Where a written report is not essential, brief the business orally. Where a report is essential, keep distribution tight, segregate the legal analysis from operational remediation, and label the document properly—understanding, as the preceding chapter explains, that a label is persuasive evidence of intent but never dispositive. The question to ask before drafting is simple: who needs to read this, and what happens to the privilege when they do.

Make disclosure decisions with eyes open. Treat any production to a regulator, auditor, or outside party as a waiver decision, made by counsel, with the consequences understood in advance. Because most courts reject selective waiver, the choice to share investigation materials with the government is usually a choice to share them with every future adversary. That may still be the right call. It should never be an accident.

Use common-interest agreements where parties are genuinely aligned. When the company and an aligned party—a co-defendant, an indemnitor, an insurer with shared interests—need to share protected material, a written common-interest or joint-defense agreement can preserve the protection. Texas recognizes the doctrine, but its boundaries are narrow, and the Texas Supreme Court has shown it will enforce those limits. *See In re XL Specialty Ins. Co.*, 373 S.W.3d 46 (Tex. 2012). Paper the arrangement, define the common legal interest precisely, and do not assume the doctrine stretches further than it does.

A short launch checklist captures the discipline:

- Scope memo from counsel, stating the legal purpose, before interviews begin.

- Counsel directing scope, witnesses, and consultants in fact.

- Engagement letters for outside counsel and consultants reciting the assist-counsel purpose.

- An Upjohn warning script in hand, with a place to record that it was given.

- A written decision on oral versus written reporting, and a controlled distribution list.

- A waiver protocol for any disclosure to regulators, auditors, or third parties.

- A common-interest agreement on file before sharing protected material with any aligned party.

Key Takeaways

The internal investigation is the moment privilege is worth the most and protected the least, and the difference between protected and discoverable is set in the first hours, not the last.

Establish the legal purpose in writing on day one, and let counsel direct the work in substance, not just on the org chart.

Warn every witness that the lawyer represents the company, and record that you did.

Decide who will see the findings before the findings exist; an over-distributed report is a roadmap for the other side.

Disclosure to the government is, in most courts, disclosure to everyone—so cooperate deliberately, never reflexively.

When parties are genuinely aligned, paper the common interest before sharing a single protected document.

Chapter 4

Cybersecurity, Data Breaches, and Preserving Privilege Under Fire

> *"There are only two types of companies: those that have been hacked and those that will be." — Robert S. Mueller III, Director, Federal Bureau of Investigation (RSA Cyber Security Conference, 2012)*

A data breach is an internal investigation run at triple speed, with more outsiders in the room and a lawsuit all but guaranteed. The forensic report—the document that explains how the intruder got in, what was taken, and what the company knew—is the most valuable artifact of the entire response and the single most contested document in the ensuing litigation. Plaintiffs want it because it organizes the company's failures into one authoritative narrative. Companies want to protect it because it does exactly that.

Here is the hard truth the recent cases teach: companies keep losing the fight to protect the forensic report, and they lose it for one reason. They build the forensic engagement for business—to find the intruder, close the hole, and satisfy a regulator—and then ask a court to treat the resulting report as if it had been prepared for litigation. Courts increasingly refuse. The privilege posture of a breach is won or lost before the breach, in how the company has arranged to retain, pay, and use its forensic firm.

This chapter builds on the two that precede it. A breach response is a specialized internal investigation, so the framework from the investigations chapter applies—purpose, structure, discipline. And the central question is the work-product question from the work-product chapter: was the document prepared in anticipation of litigation? The wrinkle here is the forensic vendor, and that wrinkle has generated its own body of law worth knowing cold.

The Law: The Forensic-Report Problem

The governing question is deceptively simple. Would the forensic report have been prepared in substantially similar form for ordinary business reasons, regardless of any litigation? If yes, it is not work product, no matter who signed the engagement letter. Federal courts phrase the test as whether the document was created "because of" anticipated litigation, asking whether it would have existed in substantially the same form absent that prospect; some courts ask for the "primary motivating purpose" of the report. The analysis tracks the anticipation-of-litigation standard discussed earlier—whether a reasonable person would have anticipated litigation when the work was done. *See National Tank Co. v. Brotherton*, 851 S.W.2d 193, 204 (Tex. 1993). The body of law that matters most, however, is federal, because breach class actions land in federal court and multidistrict litigation, and that is where the forensic report gets fought over.

Start with the cases companies lost.

In *In re Capital One Consumer Data Sec. Breach Litig.*, 2020 WL 2731238 (E.D. Va. May 26, 2020), the court ordered production of a forensic report that the company had treated as textbook work product. Outside counsel had signed the engagement with the forensic firm, and the firm was working at counsel's direction. It did not matter. The same firm had served Capital One for years under a pre-existing master services agreement; its work was paid out of the company's cyber budget before being relabeled a legal expense; and the report was distributed to roughly fifty employees, four regulators, and the company's outside auditor. On that record, the court could not find that the report would not have been prepared in substantially similar form regardless of litigation. The structure looked like business, so the report was treated as business.

Wengui v. Clark Hill, PLC, 2021 WL 106417 (D.D.C. Jan. 12, 2021), went further. A law firm suffered a breach, outside counsel retained a forensic vendor, and the firm claimed both work-product and attorney-client protection over the vendor's report. The court rejected both. It found no genuine "two-track" investigation in the record—no separate ordinary-course inquiry running alongside a distinct litigation inquiry—and concluded that the firm's real objective in hiring the vendor was cybersecurity expertise, not legal advice. Funneling the work through counsel was not enough.

The pattern repeats. In *In re Premera Blue Cross Customer Data Sec. Breach Litig.*, 296 F. Supp. 3d 1230, 1245 (D. Or. 2017), the company itself, rather than counsel, had effectively driven the forensic engagement, and the report was ordered produced. In *In re Rutter's Data Sec. Breach Litig.*, 2021 U.S. Dist. LEXIS 136220 (M.D. Pa. July 22, 2021), outside counsel hired the forensic firm, but the statement of work described an ordinary factual investigation—determining whether and how unauthorized activity occurred—and the court held that the report's primary motivating purpose was not litigation. The lesson across all four: counsel's signature on the engagement is necessary but nowhere near sufficient.

Now the cases companies won, because they show the way through.

In *In re Target Corp. Customer Data Sec. Breach Litig.*, 2015 WL 6777384 (D. Minn. Oct. 23, 2015), the company ran a genuine two-track investigation. One track was an ordinary-course factual inquiry—the kind a company performs after any incident, which Target conceded was not privileged. The other was a separate inquiry, staffed by a separate team, whose purpose was to inform counsel so counsel could advise the company. The court protected the second track. The structure was real, documented, and visibly distinct from the business response, and the protection followed.

In *In re Experian Data Breach Litig.*, 2017 WL 4325583 (C.D. Cal. May 18, 2017), outside counsel retained the forensic firm, the report went to counsel rather than to the company's incident-response or remediation teams, and distribution was tightly controlled. Applying the "because of" standard, the court protected the report. The contrast with *Capital One* is instructive: same kind of firm, same kind of report, opposite result—because the engagement, the recipients, and the use all pointed to litigation rather than business.

From these cases the decisive factors distill cleanly. Who retained the forensic firm—counsel, or the company. Whether a pre-existing business engagement already covered the same firm for the same kind of work. Who paid, and from which budget. To whom the report was distributed, and how widely. And whether the report's content and use show a litigation purpose or simply describe the company's remediation. A company that can answer those questions the right way protects the report. A company that cannot will produce it, label notwithstanding.

How Companies Lose

The failure modes are predictable, and they compound.

The forensic firm is already on a business retainer, so its post-breach work looks like a continuation of ordinary services. The work is paid from the security or IT budget, marking it as a business expense in the company's own books. The report is circulated to the board, the business units that must fix the problem, the cyber-insurer, the regulators, and the outside auditor—each recipient eroding both the work-product claim and, where attorney-client privilege is asserted, confidentiality. One report is made to do double duty, serving remediation and litigation at once, which guarantees it reads as a business document. Counsel arrives after the forensic firm is already working, so the engagement cannot credibly be recast as litigation-driven. And, fatally, the company relies on the word "privileged" stamped on the report to do work that the structure never did.

Disclosure to a regulator deserves its own warning. Sharing the forensic report with a regulator to satisfy a disclosure obligation generally waives the protection as to the private plaintiffs who follow, for the reasons developed in the investigations chapter—most federal courts reject selective waiver. *See In re Columbia/HCA Healthcare Corp. Billing Practices Litig.*, 293 F.3d 289, 302 (6th Cir. 2002). The very act that the SEC and the Texas notification statute may push a company toward can dissolve the privilege it is trying to preserve.

Consider the ordinary sequence. A company detects an intrusion on a Friday. Its IT team, working with the security vendor already under contract, spends the weekend investigating and writes up what it finds. On Monday the company loops in counsel, who blesses the existing work and asks the vendor to "keep going." A report follows, stamped "Privileged & Confidential," and circulates to the incident-response team, the board, and the cyber-insurer. When the class action arrives, none of it holds. The investigation began as business, the report served remediation, and the distribution list reads like a business memo. Nothing in that sequence was careless in the ordinary sense. All of it was fatal to the privilege.

Strategic Guidance

Winning the forensic-report fight is mostly architecture, and most of the architecture must be in place before the incident.

Build the structure before the breach. Decide now, while there is no incident, how the company will retain, pay, and use its forensic firm when one comes. The single most important decision a general counsel makes about breach privilege is made in a quiet quarter, not in the first chaotic forty-eight hours.

Separate the engagements. Maintain the ordinary business relationship with a security vendor for routine monitoring and remediation. Then, when an incident hits, have outside counsel retain a forensic firm—ideally a different firm, with no pre-existing business relationship—under an engagement that exists for the purpose of assisting counsel in providing legal advice in anticipation of litigation. *Capital One*'s central lesson is that using the same firm under the same business retainer collapses the distinction the privilege depends on.

Pay it as a legal expense. Fund the litigation-track engagement through the legal department, not the cyber or IT budget. Courts read the company's own accounting as evidence of the engagement's true purpose, and a forensic invoice paid from the security budget is an admission that the work was business.

Run two real tracks. Adopt the *Target* model in substance, not just on paper. Let the business track investigate, remediate, and satisfy operational and regulatory needs. Let a separate legal track—separate team, separate work stream—develop the analysis counsel needs to advise the company and prepare for litigation. Document both, so the record shows the tracks were genuinely distinct. *Clark Hill* failed because the record did not.

Control the report. Follow *Experian*. Have the report delivered to counsel, not to the remediation team. Keep distribution tight and need-to-know. Where a written report is not essential, consider an oral briefing instead—the document that does not exist cannot be produced. Where a report is essential, resist the urge to circulate it to everyone who is curious.

Make every disclosure a deliberate waiver decision. Treat each transmission of the report—to a regulator, an auditor, a cyber-insurer, a notification vendor—as a decision made by counsel with the waiver consequences understood in advance. Because most courts reject selective waiver, sharing the report with a regulator is usually sharing it with every future plaintiff.

The consultant principle helps, but only so far. A third party retained to help counsel render legal advice can fall within the privilege—the same principle that protected the investigative consultant in *Univ. of Tex. Sys. v. Franklin Ctr. for Gov't & Pub. Integrity*, 675 S.W.3d 273 (Tex. 2023), and that Texas Rule of Evidence 503(a)(2) recognizes for a lawyer's representatives. But federal courts apply that principle narrowly to forensic firms, as *Clark Hill* shows, because a cybersecurity vendor's core service looks like technical expertise, not legal assistance. Do not assume the consultant principle will carry a report that the structure does not support.

A pre-incident setup list captures the architecture:

- A standing relationship with outside breach counsel, in place before any incident.
- A litigation-track forensic engagement, signed by counsel, scoped to assist counsel in anticipation of litigation—separate from any business-track vendor.
- A funding plan that runs the litigation-track engagement through the legal budget.
- A documented two-track protocol distinguishing the business response from the legal analysis.
- A distribution rule confining any forensic report to counsel and a need-to-know list.

- A waiver protocol governing disclosure to regulators, auditors, insurers, and vendors.

The Regulatory Overlay

Two disclosure regimes pull against the privilege posture and must be managed alongside it.

The Securities and Exchange Commission's cybersecurity rules, adopted in 2023, require a public company to disclose a material cybersecurity incident on Item 1.05 of Form 8-K, generally within four business days after the company determines that the incident is material—a clock tied to the materiality determination, not to discovery of the breach. The rules also require annual disclosure of the company's cybersecurity risk management, strategy, and governance under Regulation S-K Item 106. These obligations force a public company to characterize an incident publicly while the forensic work is still privileged and ongoing, and the characterization must be consistent with what the company is telling its regulators and, eventually, the plaintiffs.

Texas imposes its own duties. Under the Texas Identity Theft Enforcement and Protection Act, a business must notify affected Texas residents of a breach of sensitive personal information without unreasonable delay and no later than the sixtieth day after determining the breach occurred, and must notify the Texas Attorney General within thirty days when a breach affects at least 250 Texas residents. *See* Tex. Bus. & Com. Code § 521.053. The shorter attorney-general deadline, in effect since September 2023, compresses the window in which a company must commit to a public account of the incident.

The overlay creates the central tension of breach response. The law compels the company to speak—to investors, to regulators, to affected individuals—about the same incident whose forensic analysis the company is straining to protect. Manage the two together. The story the company tells in its 8-K and its notification letters must square with the privileged analysis, and every disclosure the regulations compel must be made with the waiver consequences in mind.

Key Takeaways

The forensic report is the prize document in any breach litigation, and whether it stays protected is decided by structure set before the incident, not by the label applied after it.

Counsel's signature on the forensic engagement is necessary but never sufficient; courts look at who retained the firm, who paid, from which budget, and who received the report.

Build the architecture in advance: separate business and legal engagements, a litigation-track firm retained and paid through counsel, a genuine two-track investigation, and a report held close.

Treat every disclosure of the report—to regulators, auditors, or insurers—as a waiver decision, because in most courts disclosure to one adversary is disclosure to all.

Manage the SEC and Texas disclosure obligations alongside the privilege strategy, not in isolation; the law will compel the company to speak about the very incident it is working to protect.

Chapter 5

AI as Evidence: Prompts, Privilege, and the Discoverable Record

"Any use of AI requires caution and humility." — Chief Justice John G. Roberts Jr., 2023 Year-End Report on the Federal Judiciary

Most in-house teams are debating the wrong AI risk. The question that fills conference rooms is whether the tool hallucinates. The question that decides cases is whether the company is quietly manufacturing a new category of records—prompts, outputs, settings, logs—outside the legal department's control, then acting surprised when a court treats those records as evidence.

That is the shift a general counsel must internalize. AI does not merely accelerate work; it accelerates the creation of records, and records have owners, retention periods, subpoena paths, privilege fights, and cross-examination consequences. A prompt is not a thought. It is a document. The output your people generate, the failed attempts they discard, the settings they choose—each is a potential exhibit the other side will ask for by name.

Two recent federal decisions prove the point, and neither is really an "AI case." They are discovery and privilege cases with AI facts, and together they bracket the field. At one end, an employee's uncontrolled use of a consumer tool gets no protection at all. At the other, even disciplined, lawyer-directed AI work that genuinely qualifies as work product can be lost the moment a party tries to use it as a weapon.

For its part, the Texas Business Court recently held that certain Chat GPT conversations may be withheld from production because of attorney work product—disagreeing with a federal case that found no work product protection under similar circumstances. We address each of these cases—and their lessons—in turn.

The Law

Start with the principle that decides these cases, because the courts did. The attorney-client privilege protects confidential communications made to obtain legal advice, and it survives only so long as confidentiality holds. Disclosure to a third party in circumstances that undermine confidentiality waives it. That rule is older than the technology, and it is doing all the work.

In *United States v. Heppner*, No. 25-cr-00503-JSR (S.D.N.Y. Feb. 17, 2026), Judge Rakoff confronted what he called a question of first impression nationwide. A criminal defendant—an executive facing securities- and wire-fraud charges—had retained counsel, then used the consumer version of a public AI platform to prepare reports analyzing his defense strategy and likely arguments. He fed the tool information he had learned from his lawyers and later shared the AI-generated documents with them. The government moved to compel the documents. The court held they were protected by neither the attorney-client privilege nor the work-product doctrine. The privilege failed because the AI platform is not a lawyer and is not a confidential relationship; routing privileged information through a public tool, under terms that disclaim confidentiality, is disclosure to a third party that defeats the privilege. The work-product claim failed because the documents were not prepared by or at the direction of counsel—they were a layperson's independent research, not counsel's litigation strategy.

The most important sentences in *Heppner* are the ones describing the road not taken. The court suggested the outcome could have been different had counsel directed the defendant to use the tool, in which case the platform might have functioned as a lawyer's agent under the consultant doctrine of *United States v. Kovel*, 296 F.2d 918 (2d Cir. 1961). And the terms of service mattered: a consumer platform whose privacy policy tells users their inputs are not confidential supplies the very evidence of non-confidentiality that defeats the claim. The negative implication is the practical lesson. An enterprise tool, deployed under a contract that forbids training on the company's data and guarantees confidentiality, supports a reasonable expectation of confidentiality that a consumer tool destroys. As in the cybersecurity context, the contract does the work, and the posture—counsel-directed, bounded, confidential—decides the question.

Heppner governs the uncontrolled end of the spectrum. *Concord Music Grp., Inc. v. Anthropic PBC,* No. 24-cv-03811-EKL (SVK), 2025 WL 3677935 (N.D. Cal. Dec. 18, 2025), governs the disciplined end—and shows that discipline is not enough. There, the prompts and settings counsel crafted to interrogate an AI system were held to be opinion work product, because they reflected counsel's mental impressions about how to test the tool. That is the strongest protection the law affords, and as a baseline such materials are virtually undiscoverable. Yet the court ordered much of it produced anyway. Once a party puts its AI-driven investigation at issue—relying on it as evidence, especially through witness testimony—fairness requires the opponent to have what it needs to cross-examine. The party may not use the favorable results as a sword while shielding the rest. The court ordered production of the prompts and outputs that investigators and client witnesses used, including the unsuccessful attempts, because selective disclosure distorts the truth-testing function of cross-examination.

The court's framing should stay with every litigation leader: if you supply the numerator, the other side is entitled to the denominator. If a witness will testify that the prompts were simple, or that anyone could have produced the result, the opponent gets to test that—how many tries it took, what the failures looked like, what was filtered out. *Concord* drew one clean operational line. Prompts that lawyers drafted but no testifying witness ever used stayed protected. Prompts that lawyers drafted and then handed to investigators or client witnesses to run were swept into the waiver created by the testimony and had to be produced.

Two doctrines round out the picture. The duty of competence reaches the use of these tools: in *Mata v. Avianca, Inc.*, 678 F. Supp. 3d 443 (S.D.N.Y. 2023), the court sanctioned lawyers who filed a brief built on cases the AI had invented. The court faulted the failure to verify, not the use of the tool—a distinction that is the whole of the obligation. The American Bar Association's Formal Opinion 512 (2024) confirms that the existing duties of competence, confidentiality, and candor apply unchanged, including the duty to guard against inputs resurfacing in later outputs, and the State Bar of Texas has taken the question up through its Taskforce for Responsible AI in the Law, applying the existing disciplinary rules on competence and confidentiality. *See* Tex. Disciplinary Rules Prof'l Conduct R. 1.01, 1.05.

The Texas Business Court has now weighed in, and it disagrees with *Heppner* on the critical waiver question. In *Tate Group Automotive, LLC v. Legacy Automotive Capital, LLC*, Cause No. 25-BC11B-0020 (Tex. Bus. Ct.—11th Div. June 3, 2026), Judge Grant Dorfman conducted an in camera review of a party's ChatGPT conversations that had been withheld on work-product grounds. Defendants argued that work-product protection does not extend to a non-lawyer's chats with an AI tool, or alternatively that use of AI waived any applicable privilege. The court rejected both arguments.

On the question of waiver, the court aligned with *Warner v. Gilbarco, Inc.*, 2026 WL 373043, at *4 (E.D. Mich. Feb. 10, 2026), and *Morgan v. V2X, Inc.*, 2026 WL 864223, at *3–5 (March 30, 2026), recognizing that "work product protections are typically waived by disclosure to an adversary, or in circumstances that substantially increase the likelihood that an adversary will obtain the materials." *Morgan*, 2026 WL 864223, at *5 (emphasis added). Sharing information with an AI tool, without more, does not amount to disclosure to an adversary or create a substantial likelihood that an adversary will obtain the materials. The court found *Heppner* unpersuasive on this point.

Critically, the court grounded its holding in Texas Rule of Civil Procedure 192.5(a)(1), which protects "material prepared or mental impressions developed in anticipation of litigation or for trial *by or for a party*." That language—broader on its face than the federal standard at issue in *Heppner*—plainly covers a party's litigation-related AI conversations, even when conducted without counsel's direct involvement. Because the Texas rule protects material prepared "by or for a party," it reaches a non-lawyer's work done in anticipation of litigation regardless of whether counsel directed it.

The *Tate Group* ruling is not an unqualified shield, however. The court ordered production of certain ChatGPT pages that did not constitute protectable work product—conversations unrelated to litigation preparation—while allowing the remainder to be withheld. It further ordered the plaintiff to disclose to defendants all discovery materials or products that it had shared with ChatGPT, by Bates number where applicable, including any materials produced pursuant to the protective order. And the court recommended that the parties confer and negotiate amendments to the protective order that would make "unquestionably clear whether, how, and to what extent if so, Confidential Information may be shared with any AI tool or other Large Language Model system." The practical lesson is twofold: work-product protection can attach to AI conversations in Texas, but the obligation to identify what was shared with the tool—and to account for any confidential materials fed into it—is now an explicit part of the discovery landscape.

How Companies Lose

The failure mode is rarely dramatic. It looks like helpfulness.

A business issue surfaces—a product problem, a regulatory inquiry, a threatened suit. Someone wants to move fast. They paste internal emails and a draft legal assessment into a consumer AI tool on a personal device and ask it for the company's risk, the likely allegations, and a set of deposition questions. The output is polished. It looks like progress. They forward it to the legal department under a subject line like "FYI—thoughts?" The workflow feels informal. A court will treat it as evidence.

When litigation arrives, the discovery request now showing up in serious cases lands: identify and produce all materials reflecting use of generative AI relating to the subject matter, including prompts, outputs, settings, and logs. At that point the company is fighting on three fronts at once. It is fighting about confidentiality and waiver, because the most sensitive content was routed through a third-party platform outside counsel's control—the *Heppner* problem. It is fighting about preservation, because the AI artifacts live in places the company's litigation-hold map never contemplated: personal devices, browser histories, exported files, vendor-side logs. And it is fighting about credibility, because witnesses will be asked what they typed, what they received, and whether the AI shaped their decisions—and without a controlled system and consistent training, the testimony comes out inconsistent and the judge grows skeptical.

The cost is not merely discovery expense. It is leverage. Discovery fights move settlement economics, create delay, and force board-level conversations at the worst possible moment—when leadership wants certainty and counsel cannot confidently say what exists, where it lives, or what was disclosed to a third party. Even a company that ultimately prevails has already paid in distraction, spend, and lost leverage.

Strategic Guidance

The protection is governance, and the moves that matter are the ones built to survive discovery rather than to sound responsible in a policy binder.

First, create a legal-grade lane for AI use, and treat everything outside it as an ordinary business record. The threshold step is an enterprise license to frontier AI tools for the company and its outside firms, under contracts that forbid training on the company's data and guarantee confidentiality—the safeguard whose absence sank the defendant in *Heppner*. Then stop pretending a one-line "don't input sensitive information" rule governs enterprise behavior. Define a controlled lane for legal and legal-adjacent work—investigations, dispute analysis, regulatory response, high-risk personnel matters—where approved tools, access controls, and retention rules are clear. Outside that lane, assume every prompt and output is a discoverable business record. That framing is honest, and it forecloses the worst failure mode: everyone assuming privilege after the fact.

Second, decide in advance whether the company will ever use AI-driven testing as evidence, and if so, plan for completeness. If the litigation team intends to rely on AI testing affirmatively, assume the *Concord* problem: the other side will demand the denominator behind any favorable numerator, especially if a witness will testify to ease, simplicity, or typicality. That requires a defensible process—who ran the prompts, what logs exist, whether the unsuccessful attempts were preserved, and how completeness will be demonstrated. If completeness cannot be defended, do not build the case on the testing.

Third, route privileged use through counsel, and let the engagement look like *Kovel*. Where AI touches privileged matters, position it as an enterprise tool used at counsel's direction to assist the rendering of legal advice. That is the posture *Heppner* implied could have preserved protection, and the posture least likely to look like third-party disclosure.

Fourth, update the ESI map and litigation-hold playbook to treat AI artifacts as a data source. If the holds do not reach prompts, outputs, and logs, the company is already behind. The point is not to over-engineer it but to be able to answer, in a discovery conference, where AI use happens, what systems retain it, what can be exported, what vendors hold, and how it is preserved when a hold triggers.

Fifth, verify every AI output before it enters a filing, an analysis, or advice to the client. That is the direct command of *Mata*, of Opinion 512, and of the duties of competence and candor.

Key Takeaways

Treat AI prompts and outputs as records, not thoughts: they have owners, retention periods, and subpoena paths, and the other side will request them by name.

A consumer tool is a third party; *Heppner* held that routing privileged information through a public platform under terms that disclaim confidentiality defeats both privilege and work product—while counsel-directed use of a bounded enterprise tool, like a *Kovel* agent, stands on far better ground.

Even genuine work product is fragile: under *Concord*, putting an AI investigation at issue waives protection over the prompts and outputs your witnesses used, including the failures—if you supply the numerator, you owe the denominator.

Build a legal-grade lane—enterprise tools under the right contracts, used at counsel's direction for legal work—and treat everything outside it as a discoverable business record.

Privilege is not a label applied after the fact; if the company will not build a litigation-grade operating model for AI, the other side will build one for it, in discovery requests, deposition outlines, and motions to compel.

Chapter 6
Personal Liability Risks for In-House Counsel

"About half the practice of a decent lawyer consists in telling would-be clients that they are damned fools and should stop." – Elihu Root

For years, in-house lawyers operated on a comfortable assumption: lawsuits target the company, not the lawyer behind the desk. That assumption is now obsolete. In an environment of aggressive regulation, activist plaintiffs, and shareholder scrutiny, general counsel increasingly find themselves personally named—sometimes on substantive theories alleging securities or fiduciary violations, sometimes as a tactic to pressure the corporation into settlement. This chapter maps where in-house counsel are exposed, why the usual safety nets fail, and how to stay out of the crosshairs.

The Law

Start with the reassuring baseline: in Texas, the general counsel's professional duty runs to the corporate entity, not to its shareholders or to third parties. That principle, however, is the floor, not the ceiling, and plaintiffs have learned to build around it.

The most common route to personal exposure is the aiding-and-abetting theory. A plaintiff who cannot sue the lawyer for the company's wrong instead alleges that counsel knowingly assisted a breach of fiduciary duty by directors or officers. The theory gains force when the general counsel wore more than one hat. *In re Infinity Business Group* illustrates the danger precisely: the company's general counsel also sat on the board and ran compliance, and when the company failed, the bankruptcy trustee pursued him alongside the chief executive and chief financial officer for fraud, breach of fiduciary duty, and aiding and abetting breach of fiduciary duty. *See In re Infinity Bus. Grp., Inc.*, 628 B.R. 213 (Bankr. D.S.C. 2021). The lesson is not that the claims always succeed; it is that the dual role put the lawyer in the same dock as the executives.

Securities and disclosure law is the second front, and it has its own machinery for reaching lawyers. General counsel sit at the center of earnings guidance, risk factors, and public filings, and a disclosure later alleged to be materially misleading can draw in the lawyer who reviewed or blessed it as a knowing participant. Sarbanes-Oxley sharpened the exposure in two ways. Its officer-certification provisions place personal accountability on the executives who certify a public company's filings, so a general counsel who also holds an officer title and signs—or who is alleged to have enabled a false certification—moves closer to the line. And Section 307, with its implementing rules, imposes an up-the-ladder reporting duty on lawyers who appear and practice before the SEC: evidence of a material violation must be reported to the chief legal officer or chief executive, and if they do not respond appropriately, to the board. That duty is a shield when honored and a source of exposure when ignored, because a general counsel who sat on knowledge of a violation cannot later claim to have been a bystander.

Insolvency is the third and most treacherous front, because it is where the company's protections evaporate at the moment counsel needs them. Bankruptcy trustees scrutinize insiders, pursue avoidance and fraudulent-transfer claims, and press fiduciary-duty theories against the officers and advisers who steered the company toward collapse. *Infinity* is again the example: the forum that exposed the general counsel was bankruptcy court, and the duties that exposed him were the board and compliance duties he carried on top of the legal role.

That insolvency risk exposes the weakness in the safety nets. Directors-and-officers insurance typically covers officers and directors—but not necessarily the general counsel unless counsel also holds a covered officer title, and even then the policy language controls. Errors-and-omissions coverage rarely reaches in-house lawyers. And corporate indemnification, however generous in the bylaws, is often discretionary, excluded for bad-faith conduct, and worth little against a bankruptcy estate. The protections a general counsel assumes are in place are exactly the ones most likely to fail in the case that matters.

A fourth front is the lawyer's own conduct once a dispute begins. A general counsel who directs or tolerates the destruction of documents, mishandles a litigation hold, or is seen to obstruct a government inquiry does not merely create a problem for the company—she creates personal exposure to discovery sanctions, a disciplinary referral, and, in the worst case, criminal liability for obstruction. The duties of preservation and candor that attach to litigation run to the lawyer personally, and they are enforced personally.

How Counsel Become Defendants

Two forces turn a general counsel into a named defendant. The first is role drift; the second is tactical advantage.

Role drift is the quiet danger. The modern general counsel is embedded in the business—pricing, marketing, deal structure, personnel—and the deeper that involvement runs, the easier it becomes to recast the lawyer as a decision-maker rather than an adviser. Consider the common arc. A general counsel takes the corporate secretary title because it is convenient, then joins the deal team to move transactions faster, then accepts a board seat as a sign of trust, then signs a certification because the chief executive is traveling. None of these steps feels like a leap. But when a transaction sours and the plaintiffs arrive, the lawyer is no longer just the company's adviser—she is an officer, a director, and a signatory, and each role carries its own duty and its own liability. A lawyer who advises on a transaction is hard to sue; a lawyer who is alleged to have owned it is not. *Infinity*'s general counsel was vulnerable precisely because he was also a director and the head of compliance.

The tactical motive is just as real. Naming the general counsel is frequently less about winning a judgment against the lawyer than about creating leverage. It puts personal and reputational pressure on the very person the company depends on to run its defense. It can splinter the joint defense, force the lawyer to retain separate counsel, and manufacture conflicts. And it plays to a jury: the story of a lawyer who helped cover something up is more vivid than an abstract corporate wrong, and plaintiffs know it. Increasingly, trustees and plaintiffs name in-house counsel as a matter of course where the facts give them any purchase—especially when the general counsel also held an officer or board seat.

There is also a harm short of being named that every general counsel should anticipate: becoming a witness. Even when counsel is never a defendant, her knowledge sits at the center of the case, and the deposition notice follows. Picture the bet-the-company trial in which the general counsel is deposed for two days. Plaintiffs will probe what she knew, when she knew it, and what she advised—and the dual role hands them an opening, because questions aimed at her business decisions are not answered by the privilege. A general counsel who helped set pricing, sat in the deal meetings, or weighed in on the press release can be examined about all of it as a fact witness, with her own emails marked as exhibits and read back to her line by line. Each answer that blurs whether she was advising or deciding narrows the company's privilege and widens her own exposure. The deposition is where the adversary decides whether the general counsel is a credible steward or the next defendant—and a lawyer who blurred the legal and business lines for years will find the record hard to untangle under oath.

Strategic Guidance

Exposure is managed by the way counsel structures the role, long before any complaint is filed.

Route the most sensitive analysis through outside counsel. For securities disclosures, government investigations, and board-level disputes, channeling the high-risk legal work through outside counsel adds a layer of independence and keeps the general counsel from becoming the focal point of later claims.

Keep advising and deciding separate. The cleanest protection is role clarity: counsel advises, executives decide. Resist owning business outcomes—pricing, marketing, HR policy—because the moment the lawyer appears to make the call rather than counsel it, the move from adviser to participant is complete, and so is the exposure. Think hard before accepting officer titles or board seats that carry independent fiduciary duties; the prestige can come with personal liability that the legal role alone would never have created.

Honor the reporting obligation. Where Section 307 applies, treat up-the-ladder reporting as a discipline, not a formality. Documenting that you raised a concern through the proper channel is both compliance with the rule and the record that later distinguishes the lawyer who flagged the problem from the lawyer accused of enabling it.

Document with discipline. Frame memoranda in legal terms, keep legal analysis distinct from business commentary, and avoid the loose email chains that plaintiffs spin into evidence of complicity.

Audit the safety nets before you need them. Read the D&O policy and confirm in writing that the general counsel is a covered person. Insist on contractual—not merely discretionary—indemnification. And understand where coverage collapses, because insolvency is both the likeliest place to be sued and the likeliest place to be left unprotected.

Prepare for the witness chair before you are in it. Assume that in any serious matter you will be deposed, and let that assumption shape your habits now. Keep legal advice in a form that reads as legal advice, route business decisions to the people who own them, and resist the offhand written aside that looks reckless when it is read aloud two years later. The general counsel who writes each day as though a plaintiff's lawyer may one day read it to a jury is the one who later testifies from a clean record.

Key Takeaways

The general counsel's duty runs to the entity, but that baseline does not prevent personal exposure through aiding-and-abetting, securities participation, certification liability, and insolvency claims. *See In re Infinity Bus. Grp., Inc.*, 628 B.R. 213 (Bankr. D.S.C. 2021).

The dual role is the single greatest amplifier of risk: a general counsel who also sits on the board, runs compliance, or signs filings as an officer assumes those roles' independent duties and their liability.

Sarbanes-Oxley cuts both ways—officer certifications create personal accountability, while Section 307's up-the-ladder reporting duty protects the lawyer who honors it and exposes the one who does not.

Plaintiffs often name counsel for leverage and optics rather than recovery, but the pressure—and the cost of separate representation—is real whether or not the claim ultimately succeeds, and the usual safety nets are unreliable: D&O coverage may omit the general counsel, E&O rarely applies, and indemnification can collapse in the very insolvency where it is needed most.

Manage exposure structurally—route sensitive work through outside counsel, keep advising distinct from deciding, honor the reporting obligation, document in legal terms, and verify coverage and indemnification in writing before a dispute arises.

Chapter 7
Attorney Immunity from Suit in Texas

"An advocate, in the discharge of his duty, knows but one person in all the world, and that person is his client." – Henry, Lord Brougham, defense of Queen Caroline (1820)

Attorney immunity is among the most underappreciated protections available to lawyers practicing in Texas. For in-house counsel in litigious industries, understanding it can mean the difference between personal liability and dismissal at the pleading stage. Unlike the attorney-client privilege and the work-product doctrine, which shield communications and materials, attorney immunity shields the lawyer personally. It is a true affirmative defense, rooted in the principle that lawyers must be free to represent clients without fear of liability to the people on the other side. In Texas the doctrine is broad—broad enough to defeat claims of fraud, conspiracy, and other intentional torts—so long as the conduct was part of providing legal services. This chapter maps its scope, its limits, and its application to the in-house lawyer.

The Law

The modern Texas doctrine starts with *Cantey Hanger, LLP v. Byrd*. There, a divorce litigant sued opposing counsel for fraud, alleging that the firm falsified a bill of sale to shift tax liability in contravention of the decree. The Texas Supreme Court held the firm immune, and its reasoning is the heart of the doctrine: attorneys are immune from civil liability to non-clients for conduct within the scope of representing a client, and immunity turns on the *kind* of conduct at issue, not on whether the conduct was wrongful. 467 S.W.3d 477, 481–82 (Tex. 2015). A lawyer does not lose immunity merely because the act was wrongful, fraudulent, or aggressive; the question is whether the act was the kind of thing lawyers do in representing clients.

Two parameters define the protected zone. First, the lawyer must have been acting within the scope of representing a client. Second, the conduct must be of a type lawyers perform in discharging that representation. *Id.* The Court has since reinforced both the breadth of the doctrine and its functional, role-based focus. *See Youngkin v. Hines*, 546 S.W.3d 675, 681–83 (Tex. 2018) (immunity protects conduct that is part of the discharge of a lawyer's duties, even when the conduct is alleged to be fraudulent); *Bethel v. Quilling, Selander, Lownds, Winslett & Moser, P.C.*, 595 S.W.3d 651, 657 (Tex. 2020) (immunity can apply even to allegedly criminal conduct, because the inquiry remains the kind of conduct, not its character).

The rationale is systemic. Lawyers cannot advocate zealously if every adversary they frustrate can turn around and sue them personally. Immunity removes that threat so that loyalty to the client is not diluted by a competing fear of liability to everyone else. The protected category is correspondingly wide: drafting and filing pleadings, communicating with opposing parties, negotiating settlements and contracts within a representation, and advising a client on risk and compliance in anticipation of a dispute all fall comfortably inside it.

Because immunity is an affirmative defense, it is the lawyer's to plead and prove. Its great practical value is that it can often be established early—on the pleadings or by summary judgment—ending the suit before discovery turns the lawyer's file inside out. *See Cantey Hanger*, 467 S.W.3d at 481 (movant must conclusively establish the defense). That early exit is much of the doctrine's worth: it spares counsel not only the liability but the years of being a defendant. To capture it, the conduct's connection to the representation should be clear on the face of the record, because a court resolves the defense on what it can see.

The Limits

Immunity is broad, but it is not a blanket. Texas draws the line at conduct "foreign to the duties of a lawyer." *Bethel*, 595 S.W.3d at 657. Three boundaries matter most to in-house counsel.

The first is the business role. When a lawyer acts not as counsel but as a businessperson—negotiating a vendor contract as the head of procurement, running an operational function, making the commercial decision rather than advising on it—the conduct is no longer the kind of thing lawyers do as lawyers, and immunity does not reach it. For the in-house lawyer, whose day is a blend of legal and business work, this is the live danger.

The second is the independent duty to a non-client. Immunity bars claims premised on the lawyer's representation of the client; it does not erase duties the lawyer affirmatively assumes toward someone else. Where a lawyer makes representations a non-client is invited to rely on, Texas recognizes a limited path to liability for negligent misrepresentation. *See McCamish, Martin, Brown & Loeffler v. F.E. Appling Interests*, 991 S.W.2d 787, 791–94 (Tex. 1999). The doctrine is narrow, but it shows that immunity protects the role, not the person in all circumstances.

The third is conduct genuinely outside the representation—personal fraud, theft, or acts undertaken for the lawyer's own account rather than the client's. These are not lawyering, and immunity does not dress them up as such. The dividing line throughout is not whether the act was good or bad, but whether it was part of representing the client.

One boundary is easy to forget, and it is the one that matters most in-house: immunity runs only against non-clients. It is no defense to a claim by the lawyer's own client for malpractice or breach of fiduciary duty. For in-house counsel that distinction is sharp, because the client is the company. Attorney immunity will not shield the general counsel from a suit by the corporation itself—or, in insolvency, by a bankruptcy trustee or receiver who steps into the company's shoes and sues on its behalf. The doctrine answers the adversary across the table; it says nothing to the client on the lawyer's own side of it. That is why immunity and the personal-liability risks of the previous chapter are two halves of one picture: the shield faces outward, and the company's own claims come from behind it.

Where In-House Counsel Lose the Shield

The doctrine's role-based focus is a gift to the in-house lawyer and a trap. Three quick scenarios show why.

A general counsel directs outside counsel to file an aggressive counterclaim alleging fraud, and the opposing party sues the general counsel personally for conspiracy. Immunity applies: filing a counterclaim is quintessential litigation conduct, even if the claim is later judged baseless. Texas courts routinely dismiss exactly these claims. *See NFTD, LLC v. Haynes & Boone, L.L.P.*, 652 S.W.3d 546, 556 (Tex. App.—Houston [14th Dist.] 2022, no pet.); *Robles v. Nichols*, 610 S.W.3d 528, 536 (Tex. App.—El Paso 2020, pet. denied).

Now move the same lawyer into the business. Acting as head of procurement, she negotiates a supplier contract; the supplier later sues her individually for fraud. Immunity does not apply, because she was not representing a client—she was running a business function. The shield tracks the role, and she had stepped out of it. *Cf. Sullo v. Kubosh*, 616 S.W.3d 869, 893 (Tex. App.—Houston [1st Dist.] 2020, no pet.) (claims allowed to proceed where the conduct fell outside the lawyer's representational role).

Finally, the disclosure problem. A general counsel drafts the risk disclosures in an SEC filing, and shareholders later allege the statements were misleading. To the extent the claim attacks the lawyer's legal work in advising on the disclosure, immunity has real force. But if the same lawyer signed the filing as a certifying officer, the plaintiffs will argue she acted as an officer, not as counsel—and that argument, if it lands, takes the conduct outside the protected role. The officer title that confers status is the same title that erodes the shield. Plaintiffs know this, and they plead around immunity by recharacterizing the act—not "she advised on the disclosure," which sounds like lawyering, but "she certified the filing" or "she made the statement to the market," which sounds like an officer acting. The answer to that maneuver is built long before the complaint, in a record that keeps the legal work legal and leaves the officer's acts to the officers.

Strategic Guidance

Immunity is not only protection; it is a map of where to stand.

Stay in the legal lane. The title on the door—Chief Legal Officer, General Counsel—does not define the role; the conduct does. The broader a lawyer's footprint in business execution, the weaker the immunity, because more of what she does stops looking like lawyering.

Document the role. In mixed business-and-legal tasks, make the legal character of the contribution explicit in the record. Minutes, memoranda, and emails that frame the work as legal advice rather than operational judgment are what let a court place the conduct inside the protected zone later.

Route boundary-pushing actions through outside counsel. When the work is unambiguously legal but aggressive—hard-edged litigation tactics, contentious disclosures—channeling it through outside counsel keeps the conduct plainly within a representation and reduces the risk that the in-house lawyer is recast as a principal.

Raise immunity early, and build the record for it. The doctrine is most valuable when it ends the case at the threshold, so plead it as an affirmative defense and move to dismiss or for summary judgment before discovery begins. The motion turns on whether the record shows the conduct's connection to a representation, so the contemporaneous documents should make that connection plain, and putting boundary-pushing work in the hands of outside counsel helps frame it as unmistakably legal. Immunity proved on the pleadings spares the lawyer the very ordeal—discovery, deposition, years as a defendant—that the suit was designed to inflict.

Educate the business. If executives treat the general counsel as a business officer, opposing counsel and courts will too. Train the organization to understand that counsel advises and executives decide, because that shared understanding is part of what keeps the lawyer's conduct recognizable as lawyering.

Key Takeaways

Texas attorney immunity shields a lawyer from civil liability to non-clients for conduct within the scope of representation, and it turns on the kind of conduct lawyers perform—not on whether the conduct was wrongful. *See Cantey Hanger, LLP v. Byrd*, 467 S.W.3d at 481–82.

The protection is broad enough to defeat claims of fraud, conspiracy, and even alleged criminal conduct, so long as the act was part of representing the client. *See Youngkin v. Hines*, 546 S.W.3d at 681–83; *Bethel*, 595 S.W.3d at 657.

The shield tracks the role, not the title: conduct foreign to the duties of a lawyer—business decisions, operational functions, independent duties to non-clients—falls outside it. *See McCamish, Martin, Brown & Loeffler v. F.E. Appling Interests*, 991 S.W.2d at 791–94.

For in-house counsel the gravest risk is role drift; the same lawyer is immune for filing a counterclaim but exposed for negotiating a contract as a business executive, and an officer's certification can pull disclosure work outside the protected zone.

Immunity completes a triad—privilege protects communications, work product protects materials, immunity protects the lawyer—but unlike the others it cannot be waived by inadvertence; it turns entirely on how the lawyer acts, so the practical mandate is to advocate zealously and stay firmly in the legal lane.

Chapter 8
Cross-Border Complications of Privilege and Immunity

"Truth on this side of the Pyrenees, error on the other side." – Blaise Pascal, Pensées

State lines no longer bound the modern corporation. A Texas-based company routinely employs people across the United States and around the world, and that reach creates a hidden hazard: the privilege and immunity protections that feel automatic in Texas may not apply elsewhere. The assumption that Texas law will govern is a dangerous illusion. A court sitting in another state—or a regulator operating under another country's rules—may apply a narrower standard and strip away protection the company counted on. This chapter is about the variation across borders and how a general counsel plans for the strictest rule rather than the most familiar one.

The Law

When litigation crosses state lines, the threshold question is whose privilege law applies, and the answer can decide the case. Some courts apply the privilege law of the forum—the state where the case is filed. Others, following the approach many jurisdictions take to privilege conflicts, apply the law of the state with the most significant relationship to the communication. *See* Restatement (Second) of Conflict of Laws § 139. Either way, the general counsel cannot assume the company's home rules travel with its documents.

The domestic variation that matters most is the split over who counts as "the client" inside a corporation. Texas and the federal courts follow the broad subject-matter test of *Upjohn Co. v. United States*, under which the privilege reaches communications with employees at any level when they are gathering or conveying information so the company can obtain legal advice. 449 U.S. 383, 393 (1981). A minority of states still apply the narrower control-group test, which protects only communications with the senior employees who control or substantially shape the company's decisions. The gap is wide and practical: an interview with a line worker about operational facts may be privileged in Texas and fully discoverable in a control-group state. A communication's protection can flip simply because the suit was filed in a different forum.

The variation widens dramatically abroad, and the most important example is also the most counterintuitive for an in-house lawyer. In European Commission competition investigations, communications with in-house counsel are not privileged at all. The Court of Justice of the European Union held in *Akzo Nobel Chemicals Ltd. v. European Commission* that legal professional privilege under EU law does not extend to in-house lawyers, because they lack the independence from their employer that the privilege requires—even when they are admitted to a national bar. Case C-550/07 P, EU:C:2010:512 (Sept. 14, 2010) (reaffirming Case 155/79, *AM&S Europe Ltd. v. Commission*). The rule applies to investigations led by the Commission; national authorities applying national law may differ, and some EU member states do recognize a degree of in-house privilege. But for a Texas general counsel whose company faces an EU antitrust inquiry, the working assumption must be that the in-house legal file is exposed.

How Companies Lose

The cross-border failure is rarely exotic. It is an ordinary communication that was protected where it was written and unprotected where it was sued.

Take the routine cross-state email. A compliance manager in Dallas writes to the general counsel about a potential antitrust problem and copies a sales manager in New Jersey. In Texas, the subject-matter test likely protects the exchange. If the litigation lands in a control-group jurisdiction, the sales manager sits outside the protected group, and the inclusion may break the privilege for the whole chain. Nothing about the email changed; only the forum did.

Now take the European dimension. The same company is hit with a dawn raid in an EU competition investigation, and the Commission seizes the general counsel's candid risk memos. Under *Akzo Nobel*, those memos are not privileged, and the company's most sensitive internal legal analysis becomes part of the regulator's file. A general counsel who managed the matter on Texas instincts—write it down, mark it privileged, keep it in-house—would have produced exactly the wrong documents.

A quieter trap is the unauthorized practice of law. Many states require an in-house lawyer who works there, even one licensed elsewhere, to register under a corporate-counsel rule. Most states permit some multijurisdictional practice along the lines of Model Rule 5.5, but the requirements vary, and a lawyer practicing in a state without the necessary authorization risks not only a regulatory problem but an argument that communications from an unauthorized practitioner are not privileged at all. The mechanics of conducting employee interviews and retaining consultants so that privilege holds—the *Upjohn* warning, the engagement of consultants through counsel—are covered in the chapter on internal investigations; the cross-border point here is narrower and sharper: the same mechanics produce different results depending on the forum's rules, so they must be executed to the strictest standard in play.

Strategic Guidance

The governing principle is to plan for the least protective rule the company could plausibly face, not the one it knows best.

Assume the strictest standard applies. Draft sensitive communications as though the narrowest privilege rule among the company's operating and litigating jurisdictions will govern. A conservative assumption costs little and prevents the worst surprises.

Default to the *Upjohn* framing. Frame employee communications, everywhere, as fact-gathering undertaken so the company can obtain legal advice. That framing is the most defensible across jurisdictions, and it is the floor beneath the more demanding control-group standard. The investigations chapter sets out how to deliver and document the accompanying warning.

Plan for the absence of privilege abroad. Where EU competition exposure is realistic, route the most sensitive analysis through independent outside counsel admitted in the relevant jurisdiction, because the in-house file may not be protected at all. Treat *Akzo Nobel* as a structural fact about how legal advice should be channeled in Europe, not as a trap to be discovered during a raid.

Close the UPL gap. Confirm whether each state where the company has offices or full-time employees requires in-house registration, and register where it does; the step is usually straightforward, and the failure can be costly.

Use outside counsel as insulation in multi-state and multinational matters. For high-stakes cross-border investigations, outside counsel adds both jurisdictional reach and a clearer claim to protection than a purely internal effort can manufacture after the fact.

Key Takeaways

When litigation crosses state lines, the forum's choice-of-law rule—forum law or the law of the state with the most significant relationship—decides whose privilege standard governs, and the outcome can be dispositive. *See* Restatement (Second) of Conflict of Laws § 139.

Texas and the federal courts use the broad subject-matter test, but control-group states protect far less, so a communication privileged in Texas can be discoverable elsewhere. *See Upjohn Co. v. United States*, 449 U.S. at 393.

In European Commission competition investigations, in-house counsel communications are not privileged at all, because EU law treats in-house lawyers as insufficiently independent. *See* Case C-550/07 P, *Akzo Nobel Chemicals Ltd. v. European Commission*, EU:C:2010:512 (Sept. 14, 2010).

Unauthorized practice is a hidden cross-border risk: a lawyer practicing in a state without the required registration invites both discipline and an argument that the communications are unprotected.

Plan for the strictest standard—default to the *Upjohn* framing, register where required, and channel the most sensitive cross-border and EU work through independent outside counsel, because the protection a general counsel relies on at home may simply not exist abroad.

Conclusion

"In the field of observation, chance favors only the prepared mind." – Louis Pasteur, Lecture, University of Lille (1854)

The modern general counsel is no longer a quiet voice in the background. You are on the front lines—shaping strategy, managing risk, and often standing between the company and catastrophic liability. With that prominence comes exposure, both for the corporation and you.

This book arms you with practical strategies: how to maintain privilege in an environment where your role straddles business and law; how to preserve work product in anticipation of litigation; how to run internal investigations, breach responses, and AI-assisted work without surrendering either protection; how to recognize and mitigate personal liability risks; how to understand the scope and limits of attorney immunity in Texas; and how to navigate the treacherous waters of multistate and multinational privilege disputes.

The common theme is discipline. Privilege, work product, and immunity are not self-executing—they must be protected, asserted, and maintained. Personal liability is not an abstract risk—it is a reality that only you can mitigate through careful role definition, insurance, and the judicious use of outside counsel. Cross-border complications are not rare surprises—they are the new normal for modern enterprises.

For Texas general counsel, the mandate is clear: treat these doctrines not as technicalities, but as strategic assets. Embed them into the culture of your organization. Train your executives and staff. Use them proactively, not reactively.

In doing so, you protect not only your company but also your role as its trusted advisor. You ensure that when the storm of litigation hits—and it will—you and your organization stand on solid, defensible ground.

Appendix: Privilege & Immunity Quick-Reference Checklist for Texas General Counsel

Use this as a guide to reduce risk, protect privilege, and safeguard both the company and yourself.

1. Attorney-Client Privilege (Texas Rule of Evidence 503)

- **Significant-Purpose Test:** Legal advice must be a significant purpose of the communication, not an incidental one—and the record must show it.

- **Communications, Not Facts:** The privilege protects the communication; the underlying facts remain discoverable.

- **Label Honestly:** Use "PRIVILEGED AND CONFIDENTIAL: ATTORNEY-CLIENT COMMUNICATION" on genuine legal communications—not reflexively, which dilutes it.

- **Avoid Over-Inclusion:** Do not copy unnecessary third parties; disclosure outside the legal-advice circle waives.

- **Offensive Use Is All-In:** Putting legal advice at issue waives the privilege across the entire subject matter.

- **Crime-Fraud:** No privilege attaches to communications made to further a crime or fraud (Rule 503(d)(1)).

2. Work-Product Doctrine (TRCP 192.5)

- **Core Work Product:** Mental impressions and legal theories—absolute protection.

- **Non-Core Work Product:** Factual material—discoverable only on a showing of substantial need and undue hardship.

- **Anticipation of Litigation:** Document the moment a substantial chance of litigation arises (the two-part test of *National Tank*).

- **Dual-Purpose Documents:** Protected only if the litigation purpose is what brought the document into being.

- **Mark Documents:** "Attorney Work Product—Prepared in Anticipation of Litigation."

- **Watch the Testifying Expert:** Sharing work product with a testifying expert generally waives the protection.

3. Internal Investigations

- **Control the First Days:** Route the investigation through counsel and document that litigation is anticipated.

- **Upjohn Warning:** Give the corporate *Miranda*—counsel represents the company, not the individual, and the company holds and may waive the privilege.

- **Retain Consultants Through Counsel:** Use engagement letters tying them to legal advice, and paper the arrangement at the outset.

- **Decide the Report's Destiny Early:** Will it be privileged or produced? Structure the work accordingly.

- **Selective-Waiver Trap:** Disclosing privileged material to a regulator usually waives it as to everyone who follows.

4. Cybersecurity & Data Breaches

- **Structure the Forensic Engagement:** Retain the incident-response firm through counsel for a legal purpose, or the report may be discoverable.

- **Assume Discoverability:** Courts have ordered production of breach reports not clearly tied to legal advice; separate business remediation from legal-advice work streams.

- **Mind Disclosure Timing:** SEC Form 8-K Item 1.05 material-incident reporting and the Texas breach-notice deadline (Bus. & Com. Code § 521.053).

- **Preserve:** Place a litigation hold over breach data, system logs, and vendor communications.

5. AI as Evidence

- **Treat Prompts and Outputs as Records:** They are discoverable and must be preserved.

- **Consumer AI Tools Are Third Parties:** Using them for legal work can break privilege and work product.

- **Build a Legal-Grade Lane:** Route legal AI use through counsel-directed, access-controlled tools.

- **Verify Everything:** Independently confirm citations and facts in any AI output before relying on it.

6. Personal Liability Risks for In-House Counsel

- **Exposure Points:** Aiding-and-abetting fiduciary breaches, securities participation, SOX certifications, insolvency, and obstruction or spoliation.

- **The Dual Role Amplifies Risk:** Board seats, officer titles, and compliance duties carry independent liability.

- **SOX § 307:** Honor up-the-ladder reporting—and document that you did.

- **Insurance Gaps:** Confirm in writing that D&O coverage lists in-house counsel; insist on contractual indemnification; know where coverage collapses in insolvency.

- **Best Practices:** Push high-risk advice through outside counsel; advise, do not decide; prepare to be a deposition witness.

7. Attorney Immunity in Texas

- **Broad Shield:** Covers even fraud and conspiracy claims tied to representing a client; it turns on the kind of conduct, not its wrongfulness (*Cantey Hanger*).

- **Not Absolute:** No immunity for business decisions, acts foreign to lawyering, or independent duties assumed toward non-clients.

- **Only Against Non-Clients:** The company can still sue its own general counsel—and so can a trustee in insolvency.

- **Role Discipline:** Document that you acted as counsel, and raise immunity early to win an exit on the pleadings.

8. Cross-Border Complications

- **Assume the Strictest Standard:** Draft for the narrowest privilege rule among the jurisdictions where you operate or may be sued.

- **Subject-Matter vs. Control-Group:** A communication privileged in Texas may be discoverable in a control-group state.

- **EU Reality:** In-house communications are not privileged in European Commission competition investigations (*Akzo Nobel*)—route sensitive EU work through independent outside counsel.

- **UPL:** Register in states with offices or employees, and confirm compliance with multijurisdictional-practice rules (Model Rule 5.5).

9. Action Plan for General Counsel

- Audit privilege practices regularly.

- Train executives and managers on the legal-versus-business distinction.

- Review insurance and indemnification annually.

- Establish rapid-response protocols for inadvertent disclosures and for breach response.

- Govern AI use with a written policy and a legal-grade tool.

- Use outside counsel strategically for high-risk and cross-border matters.

Bottom Line:

Privilege and immunity are not automatic—they are assets to guard fiercely. Treat them as strategic tools, not technicalities. By staying in your legal lane, documenting properly, and embedding discipline across the organization, you protect your company and yourself.

Table of Authorities

Cases

- *Akzo Nobel Chemicals Ltd. v. European Commission*, Case C-550/07 P, EU:C:2010:512 (Sept. 14, 2010)

- *AM&S Europe Ltd. v. Commission*, Case 155/79, [1982] ECR 1575

- *Attorney General v. Facebook, Inc.*, 164 N.E.3d 873 (Mass. 2021)

- *Bethel v. Quilling, Selander, Lownds, Winslett & Moser, P.C.*, 595 S.W.3d 651 (Tex. 2020)

- *Cantey Hanger, LLP v. Byrd*, 467 S.W.3d 477 (Tex. 2015)

- *In re Capital One Consumer Data Sec. Breach Litig.*, 2020 WL 2731238 (E.D. Va. May 26, 2020)

- *In re Columbia/HCA Healthcare Corp. Billing Practices Litig.*, 293 F.3d 289 (6th Cir. 2002)

- *Concord Music Grp., Inc. v. Anthropic PBC*, No. 24-cv-03811-EKL (SVK), 2025 WL 3677935 (N.D. Cal. Dec. 18, 2025)

- *In re Experian Data Breach Litig.*, 2017 WL 4325583 (C.D. Cal. May 18, 2017)

- *Hickman v. Taylor*, 329 U.S. 495 (1947)

- *In re Infinity Bus. Grp., Inc.*, 628 B.R. 213 (Bankr. D.S.C. 2021)

- *In re Kellogg Brown & Root, Inc.*, 756 F.3d 754 (D.C. Cir. 2014)

- *In re Kubosh Bail Bonding*, 522 S.W.3d 75 (Tex. App.—Houston [1st Dist.] 2017, orig. proceeding)

• *Mata v. Avianca, Inc.*, 678 F. Supp. 3d 443 (S.D.N.Y. 2023)

• *McCamish, Martin, Brown & Loeffler v. F.E. Appling Interests*, 991 S.W.2d 787 (Tex. 1999)

• *Morgan v. V2X, Inc.*, 2026 WL 864223 (March 30, 2026)

• *In re Monsanto Co.*, 998 S.W.2d 917 (Tex. App.—Waco 1999, orig. proceeding)

• *National Tank Co. v. Brotherton*, 851 S.W.2d 193 (Tex. 1993)

• *In re Nat'l Lloyds Ins. Co.*, 532 S.W.3d 794 (Tex. 2017)

• *NFTD, LLC v. Haynes & Boone, L.L.P.*, 652 S.W.3d 546 (Tex. App.—Houston [14th Dist.] 2022, no pet.)

• *In re Pacific Pictures Corp.*, 679 F.3d 1121 (9th Cir. 2012)

• *In re Premera Blue Cross Customer Data Sec. Breach Litig.*, 296 F. Supp. 3d 1230 (D. Or. 2017)

• *Republic Ins. Co. v. Davis*, 856 S.W.2d 158 (Tex. 1993)

• *Robles v. Nichols*, 610 S.W.3d 528 (Tex. App.—El Paso 2020, pet. denied)

• *In re Rutter's Data Sec. Breach Litig.*, 2021 U.S. Dist. LEXIS 136220 (M.D. Pa. July 22, 2021)

• *Sullo v. Kubosh*, 616 S.W.3d 869 (Tex. App.—Houston [1st Dist.] 2020, no pet.)

• *Tate Group Automotive, LLC v. Legacy Automotive Capital, LLC*, Cause No. 25-BC11B-0020 (Tex. Bus. Ct.—11th Div. June 3, 2026)

• *In re Target Corp. Customer Data Sec. Breach Litig.*, 2015 WL 6777384 (D. Minn. Oct. 23, 2015)

- *United States v. Heppner*, No. 25-cr-00503-JSR (S.D.N.Y. Feb. 17, 2026)

- *United States v. Kovel*, 296 F.2d 918 (2d Cir. 1961)

- *Univ. of Tex. Sys. v. Franklin Ctr. for Gov't & Pub. Integrity*, 675 S.W.3d 273 (Tex. 2023)

- *Upjohn Co. v. United States*, 449 U.S. 383 (1981)

- *Wengui v. Clark Hill, PLC*, 2021 WL 106417 (D.D.C. Jan. 12, 2021)

- *Warner v. Gilbarco, Inc.*, 2026 WL 373043 (E.D. Mich. Feb. 10, 2026)

- *Westinghouse Elec. Corp. v. Republic of the Philippines*, 951 F.2d 1414 (3d Cir. 1991)

- *In re XL Specialty Ins. Co.*, 373 S.W.3d 46 (Tex. 2012)

Statutes, Rules, and Regulations

- Sarbanes-Oxley Act of 2002 § 307

- SEC Form 8-K, Item 1.05

- SEC Regulation S-K, Item 106

- Tex. Bus. & Com. Code § 521.053

- Tex. R. Civ. P. 192.3(e)

- Tex. R. Civ. P. 192.5

- Tex. R. Civ. P. 193.3

- Tex. R. Evid. 503

- Model Rules of Pro. Conduct r. 5.5 (Am. Bar Ass'n)

Other Authorities

- ABA Comm. on Ethics & Pro. Responsibility, Formal Op. 512 (2024)
- Restatement (Second) of Conflict of Laws § 139 (Am. L. Inst. 1971)
- John G. Roberts, Jr., 2023 Year-End Report on the Federal Judiciary (2023)

About the Authors

Trey Cox

Trey Cox is one of the nation's most accomplished trial lawyers and a leading voice in complex commercial litigation. As Co-Chair of the Global Litigation Practice Group and Co-Partner in Charge of the Dallas office at Gibson, Dunn & Crutcher LLP, he is regularly called upon to lead trial teams in high-stakes cases where the financial and reputational stakes are enormous. Contact: tcox@gibsondunn.com.

Alan Dabdoub

Alan Dabdoub is a partner at Dallas-based Lynn Pinker Hurst & Schwegmann and a first-chair business trial lawyer who represents plaintiffs and defendants in high-stakes commercial disputes. He has tried complex cases to juries, arbitrators, and judges, with experience spanning business torts, contract disputes, trade secrets, fiduciary-duty litigation, partnership disputes, and bankruptcy litigation. Known for simplifying complex cases, Alan brings trial-tested judgment to the disputes that matter most. Contact: adabdoub@lynnllp.com.

www.ingramcontent.com/pod-product-compliance
Ingram Content Group UK Ltd.
Pitfield, Milton Keynes, MK11 3LW, UK
UKHW040232290926
15471UKWH00002B/142

9 798995 296546